# SPOTLIGHT ON NATURE
# CHAMELEON

JEN FRANTZ

CREATIVE EDUCATION · CREATIVE PAPERBACKS

Published by Creative Education and Creative Paperbacks
P.O. Box 227, Mankato, Minnesota 56002
Creative Education and Creative Paperbacks are imprints
of The Creative Company
www.thecreativecompany.us

Design and production by Blue Design, Inc.
Art direction by Graham Morgan

Images by Alamy Stock Photo/Ahmed Jawid Asefi, 29, jspix, 23; Dreamstime/Ben Twist, 9, Janpietruszka, 10, Kuritafsheen, 1; Getty Images/Johan_Barnard, 11, John Mulders / 500px, 4–5, Mutebi Ivan / 500px, 17, Tanto Yensen, 27, Tim Platt, 12; Pexels/Egor Kamelev, cover, 16, Pixabay, 24, Thameur Dahmani, 29; Shutterstock/Cathy Keifer, 18, Le Do, 3, 29; Unsplash/Graphic Node, 6, S N Pattenden, 29; Wikimedia Commons/Antony Trivet, 15, Charles J. Sharp, 14, Frank Glaw, Jörn Köhler, Oliver Hawlitschek, Fanomezana M. Ratsoavina, Andolalao Rakotoarison, Mark D. Scherz & Miguel Vences, 21, gailhampshire, 28, Midjourney AI, prompted by Netha Hussain, 8, 10, 15, 16, 20, 22, Mkrc85, 6, thibaudaronson, 21

Every effort has been made to contact copyright holders for material reproduced in this book. Any omissions will be rectified in subsequent printings if notice is given to the publisher.

Copyright © 2026 Creative Education, Creative Paperbacks
International copyright reserved in all countries. No part of this book may be reproduced in any form without written permission from the publisher.

Library of Congress Cataloging-in-Publication Data
Names: Fox, Jennifer, 1976- author
Title: Chameleon / Jen Frantz.
Description: Mankato, Minnesota : Creative Education and Creative Paperbacks, [2026] | Series: Spotlight on nature | Includes bibliographical references and index. | Audience: Ages 10-13 | Audience: Grades 4-6 | Summary: "An immersive wildlife book for upper-elementary and middle-school readers, featuring a captivating chameleon family narrative, stunning photography, and educational tools like infographics, a glossary, and an index. Explores species, habitats, and conservation, making it perfect for nature lovers and young conservationists"— Provided by publisher.
Identifiers: LCCN 2025017586 (print) | LCCN 2025017587 (ebook) | ISBN 9798895810767 library binding | ISBN 9798896800293 paperback | ISBN 9798895812020 ebook
Subjects: LCSH: Chameleons—Juvenile literature
Classification: LCC QL666.L23 F68 2026 (print) | LCC QL666.L23 (ebook) | DDC 597.95/6—dc23/eng/20250718
LC record available at https://lccn.loc.gov/2025017586
LC ebook record available at https://lccn.loc.gov/2025017587

Printed in the United States

# CONTENTS

| | |
|---|---|
| **MEET THE FAMILY** | 4 |
| Chameleons of Madagascar | |
| | |
| **LIFE BEGINS** | 7 |
| FEATURED FAMILY | |
| Welcome to the World | 8 |
| First Meal | 10 |
| | |
| **EARLY ADVENTURES** | 13 |
| FEATURED FAMILY | |
| Fending for Themselves | 15 |
| Give It a Try | 16 |
| | |
| **LIFE LESSONS** | 19 |
| FEATURED FAMILY | |
| This Is How It's Done | 20 |
| Practice Makes Perfect | 22 |
| | |
| **SAVING THE CHAMELEON** | 25 |
| | |
| Family Album Snapshots | 28 |
| Words to Know | 30 |
| Learn More | 31 |
| Index | 32 |

## MEET THE FAMILY
# CHAMELEONS
## of Madagascar

Off the Eastern coast of Africa, there is an island called Madagascar, home to frogs, moths, crocodiles, and even millipedes. There are rainforests, highlands, and deserts, surrounded on all sides by the Indian Ocean. In the treetops, lemurs swing from branch to branch. They are endemic to Madagascar, which means they are native there, and nowhere else. The island is also home to more than half of the world's species of chameleon.

Like the lemur, chameleons also live in the trees. Living on the forest floor puts them at constant risk of being attacked and eaten. But when it's time to give birth, a female chameleon must crawl down to the ground. She has been growing eggs inside of her for five to six months, and now it's time to give birth. She digs a hole in the ground, where she deposits eight to thirty eggs, and then walks away forever.

**CLOSE-UP**
# Looking Both Ways
The chameleon has two cone-shaped eyes that rotate independently, letting it see two separate images —like watching two movies as the same time.

CHAPTER ONE
# LIFE BEGINS

Chameleons are reptiles with color-changing skin. From lush greens to deep blues and vibrant yellows, a chameleon can be just about any color. With over 160 different species, chameleons mostly live in Africa, Asia, and Europe. More than half of those species live in Madagascar. They live in a variety of environments such as rainforests, deserts and even up in the mountains.

Chameleons have four layers of skin: the outer later, the yellow and red layer, the black and blue layer, and the white layer closest to the body. The colors change to regulate body temperature or based on their mood. They can also change to attract a mate, or to show they're pregnant. They do not change color based on their background. This means that putting a chameleon on a polka-dot background will not make the chameleon polka-dot!

They have five toes on each foot. They are grouped together in sets, which allows them to grab onto branches as if they have thumbs. Some species

CHAMELEON MILESTONES

## DAY

- Baby chameleons hatch from eggs buried underground by their mother or are born live (e.g., Jackson's chameleons)
- They absorb nutrients from their yolk sac, climb into trees for safety, and begin their independent life

show few differences between males and females. For others, like Jackson's chameleon, males have horns while the females do not. Body size varies from less than an inch to twenty-seven inches between species. Some species live only four months, while others live twenty years.

Using their strong tongue, chameleons mostly eat locusts, grasshoppers, and crickets. Some chameleons will also eat small birds and other lizards, including their own young. They walk with a slight rocking motion, meant to mimic leaves swaying in the wind, confusing predators. In Madagascar, a chameleon's main predators are birds and snakes. Their eggs buried underground are often eaten by snakes, although it's possible for a hungry colony of ants to eat them as well.

## CLOSE-UP
## Fast Tongues

Although chameleons aren't fast, their tongues are. At the end of the tongue is a ball of muscle. When the tongue hits an insect, it creates a suction cup, and pulls the food back into the mouth.

— FEATURED FAMILY —

# Welcome to the World

After the eggs hatch, a small chameleon crawls its way out of its hole and into the open air. A baby chameleon looks like an adult, except smaller and with less color. They are able to walk as soon as they hatch. They quickly climb into the trees to avoid predators. Their parents do not look after them. Baby chameleons are often eaten by snakes and birds. In Madagascar, the flying Serpent-Eagle and Banded Kestrel enjoy eating baby chameleons. The Common Big-Eyed Snake hunts and eats them on the ground.

Once the female chameleon lays her eggs in a hole, they absorb water, and gain up to four grams in weight. Then they hatch. Jackson's chameleon, of Kenya and Tanzania, gives birth to live chameleons, and does not lay eggs. Either way, the baby chameleons are on their own. Their parents do not care for them, and sometimes eat them. These small chameleons must find food to survive.

### 1 WEEK

▸ Baby chameleons must fend for themselves immediately after birth, with no parental care

## CLOSE-UP
## A Tail Like a Monkey

Most chameleons have **prehensile** tails for gripping branches. Unlike other lizards, their tails don't grow back if lost.

--- FEATURED  FAMILY ---

# First Meal

After a baby chameleon is born, the yolk sac remains on them. The leftover sac provides food for a few days. After that, the baby is ready to use its long tongue to catch tiny insects, like fruit flies or small crickets. A baby chameleon needs more vitamins and minerals than an older chameleon. Some people with pet chameleons will dust the chameleon's food with calcium so they will grow up to be big and strong.

A chameleon's long, sticky **TONGUE** can strike prey in just a fraction of a second!

② **WEEKS**

▸ Chameleons start using color changes for temperature regulation and mood signaling

LIFE BEGINS 11

### CLOSE-UP
# What's a casque?

Veiled chameleons, from Yemen and Saudi Arabia, have casques on their head. A casque looks a little like a hat. It catches water and drops it in the chameleon's mouth. The casque helps them get enough water in a dry habitat.

CHAPTER TWO
# EARLY ADVENTURES

Baby chameleons grow up very quickly. They are often ready to mate within their first year of life. They become an adult when they reach the average size of their species. Being an adult does not depend on age, but on weight. Some chameleons take longer to get bigger, while others are ready to mate early on. In Madagascar, chameleons are ready to mate during the rainy season, from November to April. Other chameleons, like panther chameleons and carpet chameleons, can mate throughout the year.

When ready to mate, a male chameleon will bob his head in the female's direction, and he will also change his skin to the brightest colors. When the female sees the male, she will also change color, if she is interested. If she is not interested, she will hiss, swing on the branch, and turn a darker color. The darker color means the female chameleon is stressed. After mating, a female will also hiss and turn darker colors.

| 4 WEEKS | 1-4 MONTHS |
|---|---|
| ▸ Chameleons practice using their long tongues to catch small insects | ▸ Chameleons grow rapidly, developing stronger limbs and their prehensile tail |

She does not want to be with her mate anymore. In five to six months, she will lay her eggs underground.

Chameleons can be kept as pets, but they're not for everyone. They require live, healthy insects. This means keeping insects in one's home. Chameleons don't like being handled. As pets, they're meant to be watched, not played with, so they aren't recommended for children.

| 6–12 | MONTHS |

▸ Sexual maturity is reached within their first year

**CLOSE-UP**
# Three-Horned Chameleons

Jackson's chameleon lives in Kenya and Tanzania. Males have three brown horns. Females have none. Males use their horns to defend territory and push rivals off branches.

— FEATURED FAMILY —

## Fending for Themselves

Chameleons do not spend time with their siblings, or with their parents. They steady themselves on tree branches with their curled tails and thumb-like toes. These lizards like to be alone, so it's unlikely they'll seek out other chameleons until they wish to mate. Maybe a locust appears on the branch. The chameleon's eye moves to see the insect. But from the other eye, it can see a cricket. Which one to eat? The long tongue snaps out and captures one, then the other. Delicious!

**CLOSE-UP**
## Seeing in Color

Chameleons see more colors than humans, including ultraviolet light. This sharper, more vivid vision helps them spot food and find mates.

## Give it a Try!

Some chameleons also eat small birds and other lizards. In Madagascar, a larger species of chameleon might eat a smaller species of chameleon. One species is only three inches long, which might easily get eaten by a chameleon seven times its size! The larger chameleon can simply use its long tongue to grab the smaller one and put it in its mouth. Bon appetit!

# CHAMELEONS CHANGE COLOR

to control their temperature and to show moods like aggression or excitement.

### 1 YEAR

- Males exhibit bright colors and head-bobbing to attract females
- Females dig holes to lay eggs, restarting the life cycle

**CLOSE-UP**
## A Bug Filled Diet
Chameleons eat insects like crickets and flies. They stay still, spot prey with sharp eyesight, and swallow it whole. Most of their food is found up in trees.

CHAPTER THREE
# LIFE LESSONS

Madagascar is also home to the smallest chameleon, called *brookesia nana*. It's less than an inch long and can fit on the head of a match! They are the smallest reptile on the Earth, about the size of a sunflower seed. Scientists discovered them in Madagascar in 2021. It's tiny habitat puts it at great risk of **extinction**. **Deforestation** has caused it's habitat to shrink even further. Protected forests give it a better chance of survival.

In Madagascar, there is another small chameleon that has the shortest lifespan of any four-limbed **vertebrates**. It lives only four months! This chameleon, known as *Furcifer labordi,* is about three inches long, and spends eight months inside its egg. It hatches in November, and dies in April. This life cycle is more common for insects or annual plants than vertebrates. While alive, the male chameleons are particularly aggressive. Most of their lives are spent fighting over mates. Then they die, and the cycle starts all over again.

### ③ YEARS
- Adults refine survival skills
- Each chameleon tries to dominate their territory or habitat

Madagascar also hosts the chameleons with the longest life span, Parson's chameleon. They can live up to twenty-seven years. Their average lifespan in the wild, however, is around eight to ten years. An adult can reach about two feet in length. Their larger size might be related to a longer life. With proper care, they can live twenty years or more as pets.

People most often keep veiled and panther chameleons as pets. They can cost up to $800, not including their enclosure and food. Making a good home for pet chameleons can cost up to $1,500. They need the right cage, lighting, and misting system to keep them hydrated. Most chameleons are not likely to bite, but they don't enjoy being handled or touched.

— FEATURED FAMILY —

## This Is How It's Done

High in the treetops, the hungry chameleon spots a juicy insect resting on a leaf. But another chameleon has its eyes on the same meal. They stare at each other, motionless, blending into the branches. Then, in an instant, both fire their tongues like arrows, stretching nearly twice the length of their bodies. Whoever strikes first wins the snack! The slower chameleon watches as the victor reels in its prize, chewing triumphantly. A missed meal means waiting for the next opportunity. In a chameleon's world, speed is everything.

**CLOSE-UP**
## All Shapes and Sizes

Madagascar is home to an incredible diversity of chameleons. They can vary in size, color, and habitat. The Parson's chameleon (below) is one of the largest chameleons, growing up to 27 inches long, while Brookesia chameleon (right) is among the smallest, some measuring just over an inch.

**3-7 YEARS**

▸ Aging results in reduced agility and increased vulnerability to predators

LIFE LESSONS 21

Most chameleons live in the wild. As they grow up, they learn not to spend too much time on the ground—it's easier to get eaten there! They also learn to change colors, and to eat insects with their long sticky tongue. If they're careful and lucky, they'll get to lay eggs of their own, and those chameleons will grow up, too.

**CLOSE-UP**

## Color Control

Chameleons can display a wide range of colors by shifting pigments in their skin. When they feel excited or threatened, they might turn bright shades of red, yellow, or green. If it needs to cool down, they may turn a lighter color to reflect heat.

— FEATURED FAMILY —

## Practice Makes Perfect

A young chameleon inches along a branch, swaying slightly to mimic a leaf blowing in the wind. It's learning how to blend in. A bright green leaf or a patch of rough bark, every surface requires a different disguise. Carefully, it shifts its skin, trying to match its surroundings. But there's a problem. Its colors are too bright! A sharp-eyed predator swoops overhead, and the young chameleon freezes. It adjusts again, dulling its color, melting into the background. The predator moves on, and the chameleon stays safe. It still has more to learn, but blending in is a skill worth mastering.

Chameleons **SENSE** vibrations instead of hearing sound waves.

**7-12 YEARS**

▸ End of life, depending on species

LIFE LESSONS

## CHAPTER FOUR
# SAVING THE CHAMELEON

Chameleons face a higher risk of extinction than other reptiles. Around the world, about fifteen percent of reptiles are at risk. A higher number, at least thirty percent, of chameleons are threatened. In Madagascar, three species in particular—Belalanda chameleon, bizarre-nosed chameleon, and Namoroka leaf chameleon—are critically **endangered**. This is due to deforestation. When a forest is cut down, the chameleon loses its habitat. Forests are cut down for logging, cattle grazing, and "slash-and-burn" farming. Slash-and-burn farming is when people cut down forests and burn whatever is left on the ground. Then, they use the ash to help grow their crops. Without trees to swing in, chameleons have nowhere else to go. The best way to ensure the chameleon's survival is for humans to stop cutting down their habitats.

Scientists have raised money to help Chapman's pygmy chameleon, one of the rarest chameleons on Earth. This chameleon only lives in the African country, Malawi. Their forest has shrunk to less than a square mile, limiting where they can live. As a result, this chameleon hasn't been seen in over fifteen years. The money will be used to search Malawi for this chameleon, and hopefully to save it.

In Hawaii, however, chameleons are actually a problem. There are too many of them in the wild, and they are killing native insects. The species, Jackson's chameleon, was brought to Hawaii in 1972 as pets, but they were released into the environment, and now they are doing damage. They currently live on the Hawaiian islands of Hawaii, Maui, and Oahu. It is illegal to take them to Kauai and Lanai, and it's also illegal to send them to the mainland as pets. If someone does this, they can be fined up to $200,000 and possibly spend time in prison.

Humans can learn a lot from chameleons. Some scientists have been inspired by the chameleon's color-changing skin. They have created a "smart skin" that changes color in the sun. They are thinking of using this "smart skin" for **camouflage**, or for preventing counterfeit money. But there is still so much to study about chameleons. Maybe one day we'll have color-changing skin, too!

FAMILY ALBUM
# SNAPSHOTS

Chameleons can move their eyes independently, allowing them to view two different images at the same time—a true master of multitasking!

A chameleon's tongue can shoot out at speeds of up to 13 miles per hour (20 km/h), making it one of nature's fastest predators.

Most chameleons have prehensile tails that act like a fifth limb, perfect for grabbing branches and keeping their balance.

The Brookesia nana, discovered in Madagascar, holds the title of the smallest chameleon—and reptile—at less than an inch long.

Chameleons have unique eye lids that let them focus intensely on their prey while also blocking excess light—like built-in sunglasses!

Thanks to their swiveling eye cones, chameleons enjoy nearly 360-degree panoramic vision without moving their heads.

Their tongues are coated with a sticky mucus that acts like super glue, ensuring prey can't escape once caught.

Chameleons can see ultraviolet light, which enhances their ability to spot prey and recognize mates.

Chameleons' feet are structured into two opposable groups of toes, perfect for gripping branches securely.

A chameleon's tail doesn't grow back if it's lost, unlike many other lizards, so they make sure to use it wisely

Depending on the species, chameleons can live as little as 4 months (Furcifer labordi) or as long as 20+ years (Parson's chameleon)!

SNAPSHOTS 29

# WORDS to Know

**camouflage**     The ability to blend in with the surroundings

**deforestation**     The cutting down of many trees in a forest, often for farming or building, which can harm animals and the environment.

**endangered**     animals or plants that are at risk of disappearing forever because there aren't many left.

**endemic**     Found only in a specific place

**extinct**     When a group of animals or plants completely dies out

**prehensile**     Able to grab or hold things

**species**     a group of living things that have shared characteristics and that are able to reproduce with one another

**vertebrae**     bony segments that make up an animal's spine

# LEARN MORE

## Books

Bodden, Valerie. *Amazing Animals: Chameleons*. Creative Paperbacks, 2022.

Jenkins, Martin. *Chameleons Are Cool: Read And Wonder*. Candlewick, 2001.

Le Berre, Francois. *The Chameleon Handbook*. Sourcebooks, 2009.

## Websites

""Chameleons." National Geographic.

*https://www.nationalgeographic.com/animals/reptiles/facts/chameleons*

"50 Cool Chameleon Facts." Chameleon School.

*https://chameleonschool.com/facts/*

"Chameleon." National Geographic Kids.

*https://kids.nationalgeographic.com/animals/reptiles/facts/chameleon*

## Documentaries

"Chameleon – 5 Minute Documentary." Five Minute Documentaries. 2024.

Schmedes, Adam. *Madagascar: Land of the Chameleons*. Loke Film. 2013

Note: Every effort has been made to ensure that any websites listed above were active at the time of publication. However, because of the nature of the Internet, it is impossible to guarantee that these sites will remain active indefinitely or that their contents will not be altered.

# Visit

### FRESNO CHAFFEE ZOO

Known for its immersive exhibits, this zoo houses a variety of reptiles, including chameleons.
894 W Belmont Ave
Fresno, CA 93728

### MADAGASCAR

Home to over half the world's chameleon species, including the smallest and most colorful.
Madagascar, Africa

### NORTHWEST REPTILE EXPOS

The Northwest Reptile Expo is the longest-running reptile event in the Pacific Northwest. Established in 2005, it hosts expos in Portland, Medford, and Seattle.

### SAN DIEGO ZOO

Meet the chameleons at the zoo's many exhibits.
2920 Zoo Drive
San Diego, CA 92101

# INDEX

camouflage, 11, 17, 26
color, 7, 8, 13, 16, 21, 22
color change, 7, 11, 13, 17, 26
eggs, 4, 7, 8, 9, 10, 14, 17, 19, 22
extinction, 19, 25
habitat, 12, 19, 21, 25
invasive species
lifespan, 19, 20
Madagascar, 4, 7, 8, 13, 16, 19, 20, 21, 25, 28

mating, 13
pet trade
predators, 8, 21, 22, 28
slash-and-burn, 25
smart skin, 26
species, 4, 7, 8, 13, 16, 23, 25, 26, 29
tail, 10, 13, 15, 28, 29
tongue, 8, 10, 11, 13, 15, 16, 20, 22, 28, 29